JB   FRANKLIN D. ROOSEVELT
PRE   ENCYCLOPEDIA OF PRESIDENTS

14
DAY
BOOK

FRANKLIN D. ROOSEVELT

ENCYCLOPEDIA of PRESIDENTS

Franklin D. Roosevelt

Thirty-Second President of the United States

By Alice Osinski

Consultant: Charles Abele, Ph.D.
Social Studies Instructor
Chicago Public School System

CHILDRENS PRESS ®

CHICAGO

The Roosevelts' home at Campobello in New Brunswick, Canada

Dedication: For those who remember a time impossible to forget

Library of Congress Cataloging-in-Publication Data

Osinski, Alice.
  Franklin D. Roosevelt/by Alice K. Osinski.
      p.   cm. — (Encyclopedia of presidents)
  Includes index.
  Summary: Follows the life and career of America's thirty-second president, who led the country through the Depression and was elected to four terms in the White House.
  ISBN 0-516-01395-5
  1. Roosevelt, Franklin D. (Franklin Delano), 1882-1945 —
Juvenile literature.   2.   Presidents — United States —
Biography — Juvenile literature.   3.   United States — Politics
and government — 1933-1945 — Juvenile literature.
[1. Roosevelt, Franklin D. (Franklin Delano), 1882-1945.
2. Presidents.] I. Title. II. Series.
E807.084   1987
973.917'092'4 — dc19   87-17104
[B]   CIP
[92]   AC

Picture Acknowledgments

AP/Wide World Photos — 5, 8, 14, 18, 22, 32,
40, 43, 44, 47, 48, 49, 50, 52, 54, 56, 61, 69, 70,
73, 79 (top), 84, 86, 89 (2 photos)
Courtesy Library of Congress — 34, 58, 59
Courtesy National Archives — 62, 65 (bottom)
Franklin D. Roosevelt Library — 4, 10, 12, 13,
15, 17, 19, 20, 23, 25, 27, 29, 30, 31, 35, 37, 39
United Press International — 6, 9, 38, 51, 55, 60,
66, 67, 74, 77 (2 photos), 79 (bottom), 80, 81, 83
(bottom), 85
Courtesy U.S. Army — 65 (top), 83 (top)
U.S. Bureau of Printing and Engraving — 2
Courtesy U.S. Navy — 71, 72
Cover design and illustration by
Steven Gaston Dobson

Childrens Press®, Chicago
Copyright ©1987 by Regensteiner Publishing Enterprises, Inc.
All rights reserved. Published simultaneously in Canada.
Printed in the United States of America.

11 12 13 14 15 16 17 18 19 20 R 02 01 00 99 98

Franklin, Eleanor, and dog Meggie on their estate in Hyde Park, New York

Table of Contents

Chapter 1   A Crippled Nation.................... 7

Chapter 2   Little Rich Boy 11

Chapter 3   A Matter of Family Honor 21

Chapter 4   Following in the Footsteps
of Cousin Teddy 33

Chapter 5   A Minor Setback 41

Chapter 6   Relief, Recovery, Reform 45

Chapter 7   President at Last................... 53

Chapter 8   The World at War 63

Chapter 9   The Price of Freedom............... 75

Chapter 10 An Unfinished Peace................. 87

Chronology of American History 90

Index 99

Chapter 1

A Crippled Nation

A steady drizzle of rain fell on the nation's capital on March 4, 1933. While the cold, bitter wind buffeted the crowd of 100,000 people huddled under umbrellas, the rest of America sat grimly by their radios. They were waiting for the new president, Franklin Delano Roosevelt, to take the oath of office and bring relief to a country that had all but lost hope.

Not since the Civil War had the country suffered such oppressive times. By 1933 the nation had been brought to its knees by a severe economic depression. More than thirteen million people were out of work. Hundreds of businesses and factories had closed. Over five thousand banks across the country had gone bankrupt, causing people to lose their homes or their life's savings.

Few escaped hardship, and conditions were only getting worse. Farmers and ranchers in the plains states had begun to abandon their land as a severe drought destroyed their crops and turned the whole area into a dust bowl. In cities, people stood in bread lines to get food. Some of the poorest even scrounged in garbage cans to survive.

Opposite page: Scene in a garbage dump
during the Great Depression

Shacks of the unemployed in Seattle, Washington, in 1933

Millions of starving and homeless Americans lived in tarpaper shacks, cardboard boxes, or abandoned cars. Truly, the country had reached a desperate state. Even Herbert Hoover, the outgoing president, was forced to admit, "We are at the end of our string."

But on that cold March day, the strong, confident voice of the new president of the United States rang out to a disheartened nation. People began to feel the first stirring of hope that life would change. They wanted to believe Roosevelt when he promised that "the nation would revive and prosper." Yet they were doubtful when he stated that "the only thing we have to fear, is fear itself."

Franklin D. Roosevelt takes the oath of office on March 4, 1933.

The newly elected president stood on the inaugural platform wearing fifty-pound steel leg braces to support himself. As such, he stood as a visible reminder of the condition of the country in 1933. The nation had been crippled by the Depression. Its president was crippled by polio.

In 1921 the disease had left Roosevelt paralyzed from the waist down. The tragedy did not prevent him from becoming president, nor would it prevent him from getting the country back on its feet again. Americans seemed to be inspired by Roosevelt's personal courage. During the next thirteen years, they would rally around the man who had fearlessly fought against the crippling effects of a disease and learned to walk again. They only hoped he could do the same for the country.

Chapter 2

Little Rich Boy

Franklin Delano Roosevelt was born on January 30, 1882. His parents, James and Sara Roosevelt, were distant cousins. Both had come from influential and well-to-do families. His father, James, was descended from Jacobus Roosevelt, grandson of a Dutch merchant who had made a fortune in land development in New York City (then New Amsterdam) in the 1640s. His mother, Sara Delano, was descended from a line of wealthy merchant captains who had settled in the Massachusetts Bay Colony in 1621.

When James Roosevelt married Sara Delano, he was a widower. At fifty-two he was the vice-president of the Delaware and Hudson Railway. Sara was only twenty-six, the same age as James's son from his first marriage. She had been educated in some of the most exclusive boarding schools in Europe and was known in many of the prominent social circles of Paris, London, and New York.

James and Sara made their home at Springwood, a large estate in Hyde Park, New York. It overlooked the Hudson River and included several hundred acres of fields, woods, and gardens. Within these lovely surroundings, Franklin spent his childhood. An only child, he never had to compete for affection or for the things he needed.

Opposite page: Franklin, at eighteen months, on his father's shoulder

Franklin at the age of three years

As "Little Prince" of the estate, Franklin had everything at his command. He was surrounded by servants, governesses, and nurses whose sole purpose was to attend to his needs. His parents adored him and participated in all his activities. During the summers they took him to Europe, New England, or the family cottage at Campobello, an island in Canada.

Sara was especially protective of her son. She made him wear long, blond curls and dresses until he was five. Wanting to keep him close to her for as long as possible, she hired teachers to tutor Franklin at home until he was fourteen. Daily she monitored his progress in French, German, Latin, mathematics, history, and penmanship.

Nine-year-old Franklin (left) on the south lawn of the Hyde Park estate

When not being tutored, Franklin spent most of his time outdoors. He loved nature. For him it was a source of magic and wonder. Carrying a bow and arrow on his shoulder and accompanied by his favorite dog, Marksman, Franklin would spend endless hours exploring the woods. By the time he left home to go to school, he could identify almost every tree and rock on the estate.

Franklin also enjoyed tending his own garden, swimming in the Hudson River, and riding his pony, Debby, along the winding paths of the estate. Though most of his time was spent with adults, he sometimes played with neighbor boys. He never seemed to run out of ideas for games to play, as long as he could be in charge.

Franklin, age eight, with his bow and arrow

At an early age Franklin showed an interest in collecting things: stamps, birds, and anything having to do with the sea. When he was ten he took over his mother's stamp collection and continued adding to it over the years. By the time he was an adult, the collection had become world famous. At eleven, his father taught him how to shoot a rifle. He used the new skill to collect one of every kind of bird in Hyde Park. Eventually, he had a nearly complete collection of stuffed birds from the Duchess County area proudly displayed in a glass case.

Opposite page: Franklin at age eleven
with his mother, Sara Delano Roosevelt

In addition to birds, Franklin was fascinated by the sea. As a boy, he made toy boats and model ships and collected many objects having to do with the navy. With a few friends, Franklin even built a tree house that served as a lookout tower to watch for "pirates" on the Hudson River.

From the time he could walk, Franklin accompanied his father on sailing trips. At fourteen his father hired a sea captain to teach Franklin to sail his yacht, the *Half Moon*. Later James bought the boy his own twenty-one-foot yacht, the *New Moon*, which Franklin sailed from Maine to Canada.

Although Franklin and his father were nearly sixty years apart in age, James never let his age or his ailing heart keep him from enjoying life with his son.

In the fall of 1896 Franklin left his happy, secure world at Hyde Park. His parents enrolled him at Groton, an upper-class boys' school in Salem, Massachusetts, where the Reverend Dr. Endicott Peabody was headmaster. Peabody was a strict disciplinarian, instilling in the students absolute obedience to God and country. As a result of his strong influence, many boys eventually pursued careers in politics and public service.

When Franklin entered Groton, he was fourteen and already two years behind the other boys, who had enrolled when they were twelve. Franklin felt he had to make up for lost time by trying out for everything. His small size and lack of experience kept him from doing well in sports. But he did manage to make the fourth string football team and win a place on the Bum Baseball Boys team, made up of the worst players in the school.

16

Franklin (with handkerchief) performing in a school play at Groton

In other school activities, Franklin achieved more success. He sang in the choir, performed in school plays, and became a skilled member of the debating team. Later in life, when Franklin became assistant secretary of the U.S. Navy, several of his friends remembered one particular debate topic on which he had argued at Groton: "Resolved, that the United States must have a stronger Navy."

In the spring of 1898, Franklin and two schoolmates planned to run away from school to join the navy. Their dream of fighting in the Spanish-American War in Cuba ended abruptly when Franklin came down with scarlet fever. Fortunately for Franklin, his first attempt to be like Teddy Roosevelt, his older cousin on his father's side of the family, had failed. He never joined Teddy, who had resigned as assistant secretary of the navy to lead a group of American soldiers in Cuba called the Rough Riders.

Franklin
(front center)
with his Groton
football team

After several months, Franklin recovered from his bout with scarlet fever. The following fall he was stricken with a bad case of mumps. Despite his illnesses, by the end of his senior year at Groton Franklin had developed into a tall, gangly young man with glasses and braces on his teeth. He had become dormitory prefect, manager of the baseball team, and the school's best debater. On graduation day he was awarded the academic prize for Latin. Franklin proudly walked away with a full set of Shakespeare's works.

Although at Groton Franklin managed only a C average, he was well liked by other students. One classmate remembered him as "cool and self-possessed" with a "friendly and understanding smile." Reverend Peabody described him as "a quiet, satisfactory boy of more than ordinary intelligence."

Seventeen-year-old
Franklin with
his father

Groton had a strong influence on Franklin's sense of right and wrong. Under the guidance of Reverend Peabody, Franklin developed ideals that helped form his character in later life. Believing that he had a special duty to society may have led him to the White House.

Long after Franklin left Groton, he kept in touch with Reverend Peabody. Besides officiating at Franklin's marriage in 1905, the reverend conducted a prayer service for him on the day of his first presidential inauguration in 1933. Even after nine years in the White House, Franklin acknowledged Peabody's influence. He wrote Peabody the following message: "More than forty years ago you said something about not losing your boyhood ideals in later life. Those were Groton ideals—taught by you—and your words are still with me."

Chapter 3

A Matter of Family Honor

Franklin enrolled at Harvard in the fall of 1900. He and a friend moved into a luxurious apartment in a university building known as the Goldcoast. Franklin believed that nothing could dampen his future at Harvard. Unfortunately, he was wrong.

Three months into his freshman year, his father died. Franklin and his mother were heartbroken. To help herself overcome the loss, Mrs. Roosevelt moved to Boston to be near her son. Franklin, on the other hand, threw himself headlong into activities at Harvard. He had no trouble fitting in. After all, he mixed well with people, came from a wealthy family, and had a cousin, Theodore Roosevelt, who had recently become the twenty-sixth president of the United States.

Being related to the president did not always work to Franklin's advantage, however. Because of the limelight he received, Franklin was denied membership in the more exclusive clubs on campus. To compensate for his disappointment, he became a member of eight other clubs and organizations. Several visits with the president at the White House also boosted his morale.

Franklin (near front, arms folded) as a member of Harvard's Hasty Pudding Club

Franklin learned there were three ways to excel at Harvard: in sports, through academic honors, or as leader of an extracurricular activity. Franklin was not skillful at sports. He barely made it into the lightest of the eight scrub football teams, the Missing Links. His academic achievements were not much better. Because he spent so little time on his studies, he maintained only a gentleman's C average. By the end of his freshman year it was obvious that he would not excel in either sports or academic honors.

Franklin (left of center, middle row) with the Harvard *Crimson* staff

Instead, he decided he would become editor of the *Crimson*, the school newspaper. Immediately, Franklin put all his efforts into achieving his goal. By the end of his junior year, he had worked his way up from assistant editor to president of the *Crimson*. He had also earned his college degree in three years so that he could devote his entire fourth year to the newspaper.

On June 24, 1903, Franklin graduated from Harvard. Feeling the thrill of independence, he sailed for Europe alone. After a summer of socializing and charming the ladies of Europe, he returned to Harvard a confident, fashionable young man. He enthusiastically applied himself to his tasks as president of the *Crimson*.

Despite his busy schedule, Franklin still had time for romance. He began dating Anna Eleanor Roosevelt, a fifth cousin from his father's side of the family. Their paternal great-great-great-grandfathers were brothers.

One brother, Jacobus ("James") Roosevelt—from whom Franklin's father was descended—had settled in the Hyde Park area of New York. He began the Hyde Park branch of the family, and they pronounced their name "Rose-eh-velt." The other brother, Joannes ("John")—from whom Eleanor was descended—had settled in the Oyster Bay area of New York. He began the Oyster Bay branch of the family, and they chose to pronounce their name "Roo-ze-velt."

Eleanor was descended also from the Livingstons, on her mother's side. Philip Livingston was one of the signers of the Declaration of Independence in 1776. Another Livingston, Robert, had administered the oath of office to George Washington.

When Franklin and Eleanor began dating, they seemed an unlikely pair. She was a bit of an ugly duckling among the beauties Franklin was used to seeing. More important, they were opposites.

Many years later, James, their second child, described the differences between his parents: "He was tall, slender, handsome. She was too tall, too thin, homely. He was confident, personable and extroverted. She was unsure of herself, colorless and introverted. . . . While mother had a difficult early life, father had an easy one. And while mother suffered rejections from her mother, father was babied by his."

Opposite page: Franklin and Eleanor
at Campobello in 1904

Although quite different, Eleanor and Franklin were in love. He couldn't help but be impressed by her intelligence and goodness. Like Franklin, she had traveled throughout Europe and could speak several languages. Besides being aware of political and social issues, she had a deep regard for others.

Eleanor was brought up in political circles. Being the favorite niece of her Uncle Teddy Roosevelt, she was included in many of the events at the White House. This close connection to the president drew Franklin to Eleanor even more.

Perhaps what intrigued him most about Eleanor was her concern for social justice. This was one area Franklin knew little about.

Since he had never had to associate with people outside his family or his privileged class, he was unaware of the needs of the less fortunate in society. Because he had been the center of everyone's attention, he had never learned how to care for anyone but himself. For this reason, he became fascinated by Eleanor's involvement with settlement houses, slum dwellers, poor working conditions, and child labor.

As Franklin's interest in Eleanor grew, his mother's determination to change his mind also grew. She was not willing to let go of her son just yet. Sara convinced Franklin to accompany her on a five-week cruise to the Caribbean with the hope that he would forget Eleanor. Her plan worked in reverse, however. Although Franklin did have a final fling, he returned to Eleanor more determined to marry her than before.

Eleanor and Sara, Franklin's mother, at Campobello a year before the marriage

On a lovely spring day, March 17, 1905, Eleanor and Franklin were married by Reverend Endicott Peabody. Uncle Teddy made the day special when he came down from Washington to give the bride away. The wedding was an extraordinary event. It brought together at last the two branches of the Roosevelt family. As Uncle Teddy remarked, "There's nothing like keeping the name in the family!"

Obviously, the marriage was especially significant for Franklin, who by now had strong political aspirations. By marrying Eleanor, he inherited ancestors who had helped to develop New York and Massachusetts, two politically important states in the Union. In addition, he could claim family members who had signed the Declaration of Independence, administered the oath of office to the first president of the United States, and ratified the U. S. Constitution.

Following the wedding, Franklin spent the next few months completing his first-year law classes at Columbia Law School. After finishing his exams, he and Eleanor left for a long-awaited honeymoon in Europe.

When they returned in September, Eleanor was pregnant with her first child. In all, Franklin and Eleanor would have six children, whom they called their "chicks": Anna, James, Franklin, Jr. (who died in infancy), Elliott, another Franklin, Jr., and John.

The young couple moved into a small house that Franklin's mother had rented and furnished for them. Their new home stood at 125 East 36th Street, only three blocks away from Sara's own home.

**Opposite page: Eleanor
in her wedding dress**

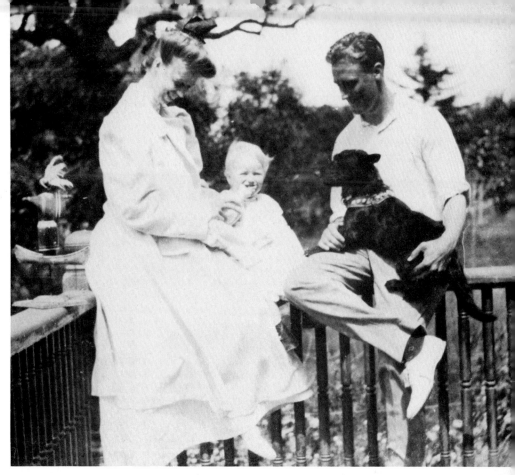

The Roosevelts in 1907 with daughter Anna and dog Duffy

Immediately, Franklin resumed classes at Columbia, struggling through the next two years with unimpressive grades and only average standing. When given the opportunity to take his bar exams at the end of his third year, he accepted. After passing the bar, he left school without completing his final year or receiving a law degree.

In 1907 he went to work for Carter, Ledyard, and Milburn, a well-respected law firm on Wall Street. During his three years with the firm, he worked his way up from an unpaid clerk to managing clerk. At twenty-five, however, Franklin's mind began to focus on other things. He was determined to launch a career in politics.

Opposite page: Franklin took this honeymoon photo of Eleanor on a gondola in Venice.

Chapter 4

Following in the Footsteps
of Cousin Teddy

In 1910, Franklin exchanged his law career for a career in politics, a step along the road to his ultimate goal—the White House. Following in the footsteps of cousin Teddy, Franklin had gone to Groton, Harvard, and Columbia Law School. Like Teddy, he intended to become a New York legislator, assistant secretary of the navy, governor of New York, and then president of the United States.

When Franklin was approached by leaders of the Democratic party to run as a candidate for the state senate, he jumped at the chance. Although his cousin had begun his career in the Republican party as a legislator, Franklin knew that he could not refuse the offer from the Democratic party. The chance might never come again.

Although Franklin was new to the game of politics, he campaigned furiously. He rented a flashy red touring car and crisscrossed two thousand miles, speaking to farmers wherever he could find them. Often that meant stopping in open fields, taverns, country stores, and feedlots. His direct approach paid off. Voters liked his flair and style. More than that, it was Franklin's promise to attack political corruption that easily won him the senate seat.

Opposite page: Franklin in 1910

Franklin as
the New York
state senator

With his first political race won, Franklin moved
Eleanor and his three children to Albany. He then
launched an all-out campaign to clean up government and
fight unethical political bosses. In New York the corrupt
political organization known as Tammany Hall had run the
city for many years.

Throughout his term as senator, Roosevelt strongly criticized Tammany Hall candidates and actively supported
reforms that would help the working people of the state.
He championed the cause of farmers and women
suffragettes, who fought for women's right to vote. In
addition, he endorsed legislation in favor of workmen's
compensation and a six-day work week.

Franklin (front left) in 1919 reviewing veterans with President Wilson (front center)

Relying on his strong support from farmers and laborers, Roosevelt ran for a second term in 1912. Midway through his campaign, however, he came down with typhoid fever. He turned to Louis Henry Howe, an ex-reporter for the *New York Herald*, for help in continuing the campaign. Roosevelt easily won reelection and from that time on, Howe remained his friend and adviser.

During his second term as senator, Roosevelt decided to support Governor Woodrow Wilson of New Jersey for the Democratic presidential nomination. He saw a winning candidate in Wilson and an opportunity for himself to become more deeply involved in government. It proved to be a wise decision. After Wilson was elected president, Franklin was appointed assistant secretary of the navy. He couldn't have been more excited. At thirty-one he had taken another important step toward the White House!

Several weeks after Franklin's appointment, the Roosevelts moved to Washington, D.C. Franklin was eager to begin the job that would keep him close to ships and to the sea. It was a childhood dream come true. Nothing could compare to the thrill he felt each time he boarded a ship. In his honor a seventeen-gun salute sounded and an assistant secretary's flag, which he personally had designed, was raised.

As second in command of the Navy Department, Roosevelt was in charge of keeping the navy yards running smoothly. The job involved countless details, from purchasing supplies to routinely inspecting the grounds. Roosevelt believed strongly in a "large and efficient Navy." This was important, since in 1914 tensions in Europe between Germany and other European countries had erupted into World War I. Many Americans feared the war would involve the United States as well.

Their fears proved well founded. In April 1917 the U.S. entered the conflict on the side of the Allies. Franklin assumed immediate responsibility for supervising the recruiting and training of seamen, procuring supplies, and overlooking naval construction. Although Franklin was disappointed when his request for active sea duty was denied, he was given the opportunity to help plan military strategy and inspect naval facilities in Europe. These experiences proved invaluable. They provided him with firsthand knowledge of navy operations during wartime and brought him into contact with the Allied leaders of Europe. Franklin would always remember this time as a preparation for the larger tasks that came to him later.

Roosevelt on an inspection tour in France with Admiral Plunkett

Following the Allied victory in Europe, Franklin spent a few months overseas attending to naval operations. He returned to the United States for the presidential election of 1920, the first election in which women could vote. At the Democratic convention, Governor James M. Cox of Ohio won the presidential nomination. To Franklin's surprise the party nominated him for vice-president.

Roosevelt campaigning for president with James M. Cox in 1920

With both candidates selected, the Democratic campaign
got under way. Franklin, Eleanor, and Louis Howe
organized an extensive trek across country by train. Hop-
ing to reach as many voters as possible on the "whistle-
stop" train tours, they campaigned at every town along the
way. The three of them traveled thousands of miles and
delivered more than a thousand speeches from caboose
platforms. Yet, the Cox-Roosevelt ticket seemed doomed
from the start. Americans wanted a change in the ruling

The Roosevelts: Elliott, Anna, Franklin, Franklin, Jr., Sara, James, John, and Eleanor

party of the country. On election day they voted Republican, and Warren G. Harding and Calvin Coolidge won by a landslide.

Although disappointed, Franklin took his defeat calmly. He had even expected it. The loss did not harm his political career, as some thought it might. By running as vice-president, Roosevelt had become part of the national scene. The campaign actually brought him to the voters' attention as an up-and-coming national political figure.

Roosevelt (center) visits Boy Scout camp at Bear Mountain in New York.
FDR was president of the Boy Scout Foundation of Greater New York.

Chapter 5

A Minor Setback

Soon after the 1920 election, Eleanor and Franklin packed up the family and returned to New York. This time there were five children, ten servants, and an assortment of pets. The Roosevelts had two households to maintain, one in New York City and the other at Campobello. Since Franklin was temporarily out of politics, he considered this an opportune time to invest in a few sound business ventures—oil, forestry, even resort hotels. In addition to business activities, he joined a small law partnership and accepted several chairmanships in charitable organizations and foundations. He also became president of the Boy Scouts in New York.

By the end of the summer of 1921, Franklin needed a rest. He decided to join Eleanor and the children, who had arrived earlier at their cottage on Campobello Island. On August 9, Franklin arrived at Campobello aboard his friend's yacht. Just a few days earlier he had caught a slight cold after battling a storm in the Bay of Fundy.

Instead of taking things easy, Franklin took his family sailing the next day. About midday they noticed a forest fire on a nearby island and landed the boat to smother the flames. Back home, Franklin went for a swim, jogged two miles, and then finished with a nice cold dip in the bay.

"In a little while," Eleanor later wrote, "he began to complain that he felt a chill and decided he would not eat supper with us but would go to bed and get thoroughly warm. The next day my husband felt less well. He had quite a temperature and I sent for our faithful friend, Dr. Bennett."

Not satisfied with the doctor's suggestion that Franklin had only a cold, Eleanor called in another physician. He diagnosed a blood clot in the lower spinal cord and prescribed massage. What a mistake! Not only was the massaging of Franklin's feet and legs painful, but it permanently damaged his muscle tissue. Only after two weeks was Franklin's condition correctly diagnosed as polio. At age thirty-nine he had to face the fact that he might never walk again.

Such a tragedy would have ended the career of a lesser man. Franklin, however, never gave in without a fight. For the next six years he mounted a courageous battle to overcome his paralysis and return to the political arena. His recovery proved much slower and more painful than anyone expected. In January 1922, his legs were put in plaster casts to prevent his muscles from slowly tightening and doubling up his knees. In February he was fitted with steel braces from his hips to his knees. Supported by the braces and with the aid of crutches (later, canes) he slowly learned to walk. Without these devices, however, Franklin could do little more than pull his body along on the floor.

In 1924 Franklin heard about a health resort in western Georgia called Warm Springs. After spending many weeks there bathing in warm mineral waters, Franklin wrote,

Roosevelt in the pool at Warm Springs, Georgia, in 1924

"I walk around in water four feet deep without braces or crutches." For Franklin as well as for other polio victims the therapeutic baths were a godsend. Realizing how important it was to provide polio sufferers with a place for therapy, Franklin bought Warm Springs. He built a home on the grounds for his own frequent visits, which continued for the rest of his life.

During Franklin's long recovery period, Eleanor and Louis Howe kept up his political contacts. On behalf of Franklin, Eleanor made many appearances at party functions. She made speeches, wrote letters, and brought home guests who represented a variety of interests. Also, although he eventually lost the nomination, she actively supported Democratic candidate Al Smith for president in the election of 1924. Eleanor had become a vital part of her husband's political career. In later life, their son Franklin, Jr., would write about their relationship, "They were a team and the Roosevelt years I believe were more fruitful as a consequence of that partnership."

Chapter 6

Relief, Recovery, Reform

No one was surprised when Franklin returned to the campaign trail in 1928. Although it took courage, Franklin decided to run for governor of New York when Al Smith vacated the office to run for president.

Franklin's disability created several problems, however. How was he going to get around? How could he present a normal appearance in public? It was important for Roosevelt to show that his handicap would not affect his ability to carry out the duties of high office.

Louis Howe, now Roosevelt's campaign manager, established two campaign rules. First, Franklin should never be carried in public. Second, the press should not be allowed to photograph Franklin from the waist down. For campaigning, Franklin was given a custom-made automobile that had special hand controls.

The care taken in this campaign to show Roosevelt's ability as a politician certainly paid off. He defeated the Republican candidate for governor by 25,564 votes. Other Democratic candidates in the 1928 elections did not do as well. The biggest loss was for the office of president, with Al Smith losing to the Republican Herbert Hoover.

Opposite page: Roosevelt arrives at
Hyde Park Town Hall to vote in 1928

Although Roosevelt had won the governorship by a narrow margin, he was thrilled about his political victory. At last he had reached one of the most significant steps on his road to the White House.

On January 1, 1929, Franklin was sworn in as governor of New York. He took his oath of office in the same room where Teddy Roosevelt had been sworn in when he became governor thirty years before.

Franklin served two terms as governor. During his tenure he fought for reforms in agriculture, conservation, and labor. Legislation that he supported provided tax relief for farmers, reforestation of abandoned farmland, old-age pensions, a forty-eight hour work week for women, and prison reform.

It was clear that reform was needed. In October 1929 the stock market crashed, ushering in the severest economic depression the United States and the rest of the world had ever seen. Few people had anticipated the disaster. Everyone had been too busy enjoying the prosperous times of the early 1920s.

During those years, factories were producing goods at an alarming rate. Everyone was buying on credit. Although little money was circulating, stores provided easy credit terms for their customers. Banks were practically giving money away at low interest rates. With the "Buy Now, Pay Later" plan, who could resist?

Before long, most households in America owned at least one new electrical appliance. In addition, a great number of people had money in the bank or owned stock in some corporation.

Opposite page: Governor and
Mrs. Roosevelt in Warm Springs

Depositors outside the closed doors of their bank in New York in 1931

Like other purchases, stocks were bought on credit. Many were bought "on margin"; that is, customers paid a small down payment for their stock, intending to pay the rest when the stock was resold at a profit.

No one would deny that wealth was being made during the period called the "Roaring Twenties." However, that wealth was not equally distributed. A national study done in 1929 showed that three-fifths of the nation's wealth was owned by only 2 percent of the population. The rich were getting richer, and the poor were getting poorer. Although some industries were flourishing, others were in trouble. Railroads, coal mining, and agriculture were suffering serious problems. The common workers carried the heaviest credit and tax burdens.

Roosevelt reading letters of congratulation after being elected governor of New York

When the stock market crashed in 1929, the entire country—many rich and poor alike—went bankrupt. Banks closed, businesses failed, and millions of people lost all their money and found themselves out of work. Cities with large populations, such as New York City, were the hardest hit. As governor of New York, Franklin Roosevelt took immediate action. He set up a state relief program that became a model for other states. The program provided jobs in conservation and unemployment insurance. Many of the policies and practices he initiated as governor, Roosevelt used later as president. He focused, both as governor and later as president, on the plight of the poor.

Roosevelt next to a campaign poster

After two terms as governor, Franklin realized that his economic programs should be tried on a national scale. The country sorely needed relief. On January 23, 1932, one week before his fiftieth birthday, he formally announced that he would run for president. In July he flew to Chicago to accept the Democratic nomination. The convention hall swelled with the sound of his theme song, "Happy Days Are Here Again," as excited crowds cheered his arrival. When Franklin spoke, he outlined his program for recovery and pledged "a new deal for the American people."

Roosevelt with his friend and aide, Louis Howe

Following the convention, FDR, as the press liked to call him, set out on a grueling cross-country tour. Although he was the clear favorite in the race, Roosevelt did not want to take any chances that President Herbert Hoover would be reelected. Carefully sticking to the issues, he reminded voters that Hoover—as well as Congress—had done little in three years to ease the Depression. As a result, he said, the country needed immediate relief: farm price stabilization, a public works program, a conservation program, and a system of unemployment insurance.

Voters believed FDR's programs were worth a try, and in November they elected him president. Roosevelt carried 42 of the 48 states, 472 electoral votes to Hoover's 59, and 22,815,539 popular votes to Hoover's 15,750,000. Clearly, the country had given FDR a mandate. By electing him in the worst months of the Depression, they were saying: "You have given us hope, now give us bread."

Chapter 7

President at Last

On March 4, 1933, Franklin Delano Roosevelt was formally sworn in as the thirty-second president of the United States. Unlike other politicians who had lost their ability to lead in these troubled times, the new president showed confidence and determination.

In his inaugural address, Roosevelt told the American people exactly what he intended to do and how he intended to do it. He said that his first task was to put people to work and bring relief to the homeless. Before creating jobs, however, he would ask Congress for "strict supervision of all banking, credits, and investments." This, he believed, would temporarily stabilize the banks.

Roosevelt acted quickly. The day after his inauguration, he called his cabinet together and told them he would ask Congress to hold an emergency session on March 9.

In the meantime, he declared a nationwide "bank holiday." This measure closed all banks and suspended their transactions for four days until Congress could enact legislation that would revive the banks. Within that week the Emergency Banking Act was signed into law. By the end of the month, three-fourths of all banks in the Federal Reserve System were reopened.

Hundreds line up for food from a New York City relief kitchen in 1934.

Franklin always kept the American people informed about the changes he was making in the government. Only eight days after taking office, he began Sunday evening radio broadcasts from the White House. His first broadcast set the stage for dozens of others he would deliver during his administration: "My friends, I want to talk for a few minutes about banking. I want to tell you what has been done in the last few days, why it was done, and what the next steps are going to be . . . ." After explaining his course of action, he usually ended by including his audience in his efforts, saying "Together we cannot fail." These "Fireside Chats," as they were called, made each American feel as if he or she were a partner in the great task of running the country.

Roosevelt signs an emergency banking bill on March 9, 1933.

Roosevelt was so successful in passing his first banking bill that he decided to keep Congress in session. For the next several months, he pushed through as many reform bills as possible. This special session of Congress, which met from March 9 to June 16, was called the "Hundred Days." It is often considered the most extraordinary session of Congress in America's history. Not since the founding of our country has more legislation been passed in such a short time with such lasting effects.

Women working on a canning project sponsored by the WPA

Roosevelt called the reform bills passed during that session the New Deal. The legislation established many agencies, often referred to only by their initials. Most were created to provide jobs. The Civilian Conservation Corps (CCC), one of Roosevelt's favorite programs, employed hundreds of thousands of people to reforest public land, build flood-control structures, and improve national parks. The Public Works Administration (PWA) put the jobless to work on large-scale construction, highway, and other public projects. Between 1933 and 1939 several thousand schools were built throughout the country. The largest PWA projects included the Grand Coulee Dam in Washington State, the Triborough Bridge in New York, and the entire sewage system in Chicago.

At the heart of early New Deal programs were the Agricultural Adjustment Agency (AAA) and the National Recovery Administration (NRA). The AAA limited farm production and actually paid farmers not to grow certain crops. By limiting production, the government could control prices. Of all the New Deal legislation, perhaps the most far-reaching was the NRA bill. It guaranteed a minimum wage and a limited number of working hours, and it encouraged the right of workers to join unions.

Early in 1935, New Deal programs began to focus on the long-term rehabilitation of the country. One agency, the Tennessee Valley Authority (TVA), provided flood control and cheap hydroelectric power for several states. Through the TVA, fifty-one multipurpose dams were built on the Tennessee River. Important legislation was created for business and labor. The Federal Deposit Insurance Corporation (FDIC) provided federal insurance for all bank deposits under $5,000. The Securities and Exchange Commission (SEC) controlled the stock market. The Social Security Act provided for old-age pensions and welfare for the needy, disabled, blind, and unemployed.

Of all the New Deal job programs, the Works Projects Administration (WPA) employed the most people. On an average, the agency hired about 2.1 million people each year to perform a variety of tasks ranging from digging ditches to writing plays. The WPA paid artists to paint murals on public buildings and paid actors to put on free theatrical productions. Parks were cleaned up across the country. The WPA even financed large-scale projects like the construction of La Guardia Airport in New York.

A cartoon from the New Deal era

Slowly, FDR's programs were improving the condition of the country. By November 1936, when he was up for reelection, unemployment was down and banks were more secure. Although the Depression still dragged on, most Americans believed in what the president was doing. Farmers, laborers, and the underprivileged gave him their full support. He was reelected by a wide margin. During FDR's second term in office, however, cracks began to appear in the solid foundation he had built.

Feeling that too much power had been given to the president, the Supreme Court declared several of his New Deal programs unconstitutional. His policies were getting criticism from the business community as well as the press. And Roosevelt's plan to "pack the courts" infuriated his enemies and began turning away fellow Democrats.

OLD RELIABLE!

A cartoon knocking Roosevelt's lavish spending on government programs

Since becoming president, Roosevelt had not had an opportunity to appoint any Supreme Court justices himself. Believing that the court was standing in the way of the nation's economic recovery, Roosevelt proposed that the number of judges be increased from nine to fifteen. He then would be able to appoint six new judges of his own choosing. In effect, the president would be packing the court with judges who shared his beliefs and supported his policies. Fortunately, Congress rejected this plan. The event, however, left a lasting black mark on Roosevelt's administration.

Eleanor at a camp for unemployed women, opened at the suggestion of herself and Secretary of Labor Frances Perkins

Eleanor Roosevelt's activities brought further concern from conservative Democrats. She was criticized for traveling too much and being too outspoken. More than any other First Lady, Eleanor actively supported civil rights and the causes of the underprivileged. As a result of her influence, there were twenty blacks serving in various government advisory posts by 1938. These included a woman, Mary McLeod Bethune, who was special adviser on minority affairs. Frances Perkins, the first woman to serve in a president's cabinet, had been appointed secretary of labor in 1933.

A 1940 campaign parade down Seventh Avenue in New York City

Despite the problems troubling Roosevelt during his second term as president, Americans voted him in for a third term in 1940. Most people seemed to feel secure with Roosevelt's leadership. Some were afraid that a new president would reverse the progress the country had made so far. Others were concerned about the outbreak of war in Europe and the Far East. For whatever reason, voters elected FDR for another four years. But the president had little time to celebrate his victory. His attention turned to events in Europe and Asia where an ever-widening war was entering its second year.

Chapter 8

The World at War

By 1930 many countries in Europe and Asia were ruled by strong dictators. These rulers had built up massive armies and navies and had begun to conquer neighboring countries. In 1940 Japan, Italy, and Germany formed a pact to help each other build their great empires and divide the world among them. These three countries were called the Axis powers.

The first of these dictators' invasions began in 1931 when Japan marched into Manchuria and claimed it. On the other side of the world, Benito Mussolini, the dictator of Italy, conquered Ethiopia in 1935 and Albania in 1939. Meanwhile, the powerful dictator of Germany, Adolf Hitler, was building an empire he called the Third Reich. Hitler had become leader of Germany by proposing a plan to restore its economy and to make the country the most powerful nation in the world. Through the National Socialist Workers (Nazi) party, he gradually eliminated anyone who opposed him and took complete control of the country. Hitler planned to create a master race of people called Aryans to dominate the world. Anyone who was not of Aryan ancestry or who did not support Nazi ideas would be eliminated.

Opposite page: Grumann Wildcats
on a mission in the Pacific

In 1938 Hitler began extending his powerful empire. Without warning, Nazi troops marched into Austria and occupied it. Then in 1939, Germany acquired Czechoslovakia through an agreement with other European powers, who wanted to avoid war with Germany. Their hopes were dashed when Hitler invaded Poland in September 1939. This invasion was the event that marked the beginning of World War II.

At first the German army smashed all resistance. By May 1940, Norway, Denmark, The Netherlands, Belgium, and Luxembourg were under German control. Jews, whom Hitler blamed for the Depression, as well as anyone opposing Nazi rule, were taken to concentration camps where they were killed. More than six million Jews and people who resisted the Nazis were tortured and starved to death. The greatest number of people died in gas chambers. Eventually, when news of the death camps began leaking out, no one wanted to believe it. How could something so horrible be true?

Several countries resisted Hitler's advance across Europe, but they were overpowered by the strength of his armies. Others tried to reason with him but were fooled by his promises.

Countries like the United States, who were not in the direct path of Hitler's expansion, remained neutral. They did not want to get involved in another world war. But when Great Britain and France declared war on Germany in 1939, the United States was forced to support its allies in Europe. The conflict threatened to engulf the entire continent.

Right: A photo of Adolf Hitler from the photo collection of his friend Eva Braun

Below: Jews are marched out of their ghetto under the guns of German commandos.

German troops enter Paris a few days before France fell to Germany.

Throughout 1940 the Axis nations continued to expand their power. On June 10, Italy declared war on France and Great Britain. German troops entered Paris four days later, and on June 22 France surrendered. By November 1942, German troops occupied all of France.

Following the defeat of France, only the British remained to fight the aggressors. And fight they did. Every night for two solid months, German airplanes bombed London. During the day Britain's small but highly skilled Royal Air Force (RAF) fought back. These pilots destroyed so many German planes that Hitler called off the invasion of Britain.

Roosevelt and Winston Churchill

As soon as France fell, Roosevelt came to Britain's aid. In August he met with Winston Churchill, the prime minister of England. Together they agreed on war aims and wrote a program for peace called the Atlantic Charter. The charter outlined how peace was to be restored when Nazi Germany was defeated. At the same time, Roosevelt promised Churchill shipments of ammunition, weapons, and destroyers.

Following his meeting with Churchill, Roosevelt called for the first peacetime draft in the United States. The Selective Training and Service Act registered sixteen million American men between the ages of twenty-one and thirty-five for the armed services.

Roosevelt then scheduled another Fireside Chat with the American people. This time he wished to explain the new lend-lease policy that he was going to ask Congress to pass. Although he promised to keep America out of the war, he said it was necessary to lend, lease, or sell arms and other goods to "any country whose defense was vital to the United States."

The enemy could not be reasoned with, he declared in concluding his address. "The experience of the past two years has proven beyond doubt that no nation can appease the Nazis. No man can tame a tiger into a kitten by stroking it."

Roosevelt assured Americans that European countries that were defending themselves from the enemy were not asking the United States to do their fighting for them. Rather, he said, they were asking Americans for "the implements of war, the planes, the tanks, the guns, the freighters which will enable them to fight for their liberty and for our security."

For the first time, Roosevelt referred to America as the "Arsenal of Democracy." He meant that America had a responsibility to provide weapons and other supplies to countries that were fighting to maintain their freedom and their democratic way of life. For Europeans, America was their only hope.

Premier Josef Stalin of the Soviet Union

Three months after Roosevelt's Fireside Chat, Congress passed the Lend-Lease Act. It allowed the United States to offer massive wartime aid to England and France. Within a few months America was giving aid to the Soviet Union as well. Russia was attacked by Germany in June 1941, even though Hitler had signed a treaty of friendship only a few months before with Premier Josef Stalin, the leader of the Soviet Union.

Japan's Premier Hideki Tojo, who led Japan into war with the United States

Although the lend-lease policy strengthened the Allies, it widened the gap between the United States and the Axis powers. The president's most immediate concern lay with Japan. Relations with the Far Eastern nation had been deteriorating since France surrendered to Germany in 1940. Japan took advantage of this situation by taking possession of French Indochina (now Vietnam). Outraged by the aggression, the U.S. stopped all trade with Japan and cut off its vital shipments of oil. Japan interpreted this as the action of an enemy and decided to retaliate. Secretly,

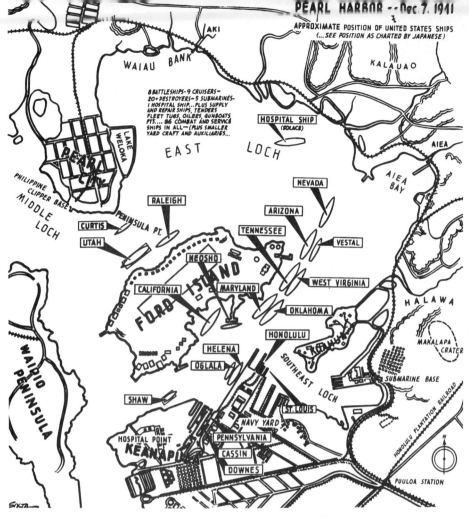

Map of Pearl Harbor, showing approximate positions of U.S. ships

Japan began making plans to occupy all American and British possessions in Southeast Asia and the Pacific Ocean. With these key bases under its control, Japan knew that the United States would not be able to defend itself in a war with Japan.

America's naval and air base at Pearl Harbor in the Hawaiian Islands was chosen as the site of the first attack. On November 26, 1941, thirty-three Japanese ships sailed for Hawaii. Twelve days later they stopped 220 miles from Oahu and launched 350 planes from carriers.

A U.S. naval ship burns after the attack by Japanese aircraft.

At 7:55 A.M. on Sunday, December 7, people on Oahu were awakened by the roar of Japanese planes overhead. Radiomen clicked out a message at 7:58 A.M.: "AIR RAID, PEARL HARBOR. THIS IS NOT DRILL!" It was too late. The Americans were caught off guard. Horrified sailors awoke to find their ships in flames and sinking. The men who managed to reach aircraft and guns not yet destroyed were hindered by the smoke and confusion. After nearly two hours of steady bombing, the Japanese planes disappeared into the smoke-filled sky. Their target lay in ruins. Eight American battleships, three cruisers, three destroyers, and four other craft were either sunk or severely damaged. More than 170 planes were lost and more than 3,500 men were killed or wounded.

The Naval Air Station at Pearl Harbor on the morning of December 7, 1941

At 1:40 in the afternoon, President Roosevelt was notified of the attack. Shaken by the news, he knew what he had to do. The next morning he addressed Congress as millions of stunned Americans listened on their radios.

"Yesterday," he began gravely, "December 7, 1941 — a date which will live in infamy — the United States of America was suddenly and deliberately attacked by naval and air forces of the Empire of Japan . . . . I ask that Congress declare that since the unprovoked and dastardly attack by Japan . . . , a state of war has existed between the United States and the Japanese Empire."

It took only thirty-three minutes for Congress to vote for a declaration of war. On the same day, England and Canada declared war on Japan. Three days later, on December 11, 1941, Germany and Italy declared war on the United States. America had now officially entered World War II on both sides of the world.

Chapter 9

The Price of Freedom

The attack on Pearl Harbor united the country as nothing else could have. Within that week thousands of men enlisted in the armed forces. For the first time, women were allowed to volunteer. Of the 300,000 who enlisted, all were restricted to women's units. Blacks and Japanese-Americans also served in the armed forces, but in separate units. The war did little to change the racial divisions that existed in much of the country.

Those suffering the greatest discrimination during the war were citizens of Japanese descent. After the attack on Pearl Harbor, people on the West Coast feared that Japanese-Americans would support Japan and act as spies or saboteurs against the United States. To prevent mass hysteria, Roosevelt ordered army personnel to remove "any or all persons" of Japanese descent from areas of the U.S. mainland designated as "military zones."

By the end of 1942, more than 110,000 Japanese Americans—two-thirds of them native-born citizens—were imprisoned in "relocation centers." Most were kept there until the end of the war. The camps, which were surrounded by barbed-wire fences and guarded by armed troops, were located in regions such as the deserts of California and Arizona and the swamplands of Arkansas.

Opposite page: President Roosevelt
making a radio broadcast during the war

In spite of the discrimination the Japanese endured, more than a thousand young men, whose parents remained in the camps, volunteered for military service. Their regiment, known as the Nisei or the 442nd, suffered more casualties and won more medals than any other army combat unit.

Roosevelt knew that the victory he promised Americans would depend first of all on their ability to produce massive amounts of war materials. They did not disappoint him. In rapid succession, companies changed from peacetime to wartime production. They employed thousands of women to replace the men who had gone to war. Shipyard crews worked day and night. Some factories never closed, while the nation's farmers doubled their output. Even children did their part by collecting scrap metal and rubber. In less than three years, Americans were producing more weapons and supplies than all the Axis countries combined. In addition, they had built the world's largest, most powerful naval force.

While factories were turning out the implements of war, the president was meeting with Allied leaders to discuss war strategy. Roosevelt was responsible for resolving differences among the Allied leaders and for keeping them together. This was an enormous task, since each country had different motives for fighting the war. Two Allied countries, Russia and China, wanted to run their own war operations. The United States and Great Britain, however, decided to work closely together. During the war Roosevelt and Prime Minister Churchill met at least ten times to cooperate on war efforts.

Above: Japanese-Americans lined up for inspection at a relocation center
Below: Relocated Japanese helping to relieve the farm labor shortage

Although the war raged on two fronts—Europe and Asia—the Allies agreed that Hitler and Mussolini should be dealt with first. Once the enemy in Europe was defeated, they could combine forces against Japan. For several of the Allies, this was a difficult decision to uphold. From December 1941 through June 1942, Allied outposts in the Pacific fell to the Japanese, one after the other—Guam, Wake Island, Hong Kong, Malaya, and the Philippines. Early in 1942, when the Allies launched a counterattack, the Japanese empire stretched from the East Indies to parts of Alaska's Aleutian Islands.

Lieutenant Colonel James H. Doolittle led a daring bombing raid on Tokyo and other Japanese cities in April 1942. Next, Admiral Chester Nimitz (commander of the Pacific fleet) and General Douglas MacArthur (commander of U.S. Army forces in the Far East) directed the offensive at such famous battle sites as the Coral Sea, Midway, Guadalcanal, Leyte Gulf, and the Philippines. With control of the Philippines, the Allies had gained an important base from which they could supply their combat lines.

Allied efforts to free the European continent from the Axis began in North Africa. Operation Torch, the code name for the invasion of North Africa, was designed to force the Axis armies out of Africa and clear the way for an invasion of Italy from the south. The plan worked. In November 1942, American and British troops commanded by Lieutenant General Dwight D. Eisenhower landed on the coast of Algeria and Morocco. After six months of shrewd maneuvering and intense fighting, they forced a German surrender.

Above: Benito Mussolini reviews troops on the Yugoslav border.
Below: Roosevelt observes maneuvers of a tank unit in French Morocco.

This company of black Americans in Italy wiped out several machine gun nests.

Months later the Allies invaded Italy. Beginning in July 1943, they struggled through mud, mountains, and snow, enduring months of grueling warfare at such places as Salerno and Anzio. Finally, on May 2, 1945, the German forces in Italy surrendered, four days after Mussolini had been shot. Once the Allies occupied Italy, they began their drive north to Hitler's stronghold. While they pushed north towards Germany, Russians fought their way west towards the same rendezvous point.

Winston Churchill, Franklin D. Roosevelt, and Josef Stalin at Yalta, February 1945

Meanwhile, in December, the three Allied leaders met in the Iranian capital of Tehran to discuss their final strategy against Germany. At the conference Roosevelt, Stalin, and Churchill pledged to support a new international peacekeeping organization, known eventually as the United Nations, that would be established after the war. The Allies also agreed that the invasion to end the war in Europe should take place at Normandy, France.

On the morning of June 6, 1944 (D-Day), the long-awaited cross-channel invasion, codenamed Operation Overlord, got under way. Almost two million British, Canadian, American, and French troops took part in the largest land and sea invasion ever attempted. Commanded by General Dwight Eisenhower, 9,000 ships and small landing craft and more than 11,000 aircraft surprised the German stronghold. For ten months the Allies fought their way toward Berlin. As the Russians drove from the east, Allied forces advanced from the west.

In January 1945, while the battles raged, Roosevelt was sworn in for a fourth term as president. He was tired and would have preferred to leave the presidency, as his note to the Democratic national chairman in 1944 implies: "All that is in me cries out to go back to my home on the Hudson River, but we of this generation chance to live in a day and hour when our nation has been attacked, and when its future existence and the future existence of our chosen method of government are at stake."

A month after his inauguration, Roosevelt, in poor health and worn out from the burdens of global war, met with Stalin and Churchill at Yalta, Russia. They discussed the final assault on Germany and planned for its occupation after the war. They also decided to meet late in April in San Francisco to draft the United Nations charter.

Roosevelt left Yalta in need of a well-deserved rest. The pressures were finally taking their toll on him. By age sixty-two, his vast supply of energy had dwindled. Eleanor remarked to a relative that "FDR says he feels much better but I don't think he longs to get back and fight."

Above: American assault troops pour onto the coast of France in June 1944.
Below: President Roosevelt on his fourth inauguration day, January 20, 1945

Roosevelt and his vice-president, Harry Truman

The responsibilities of his office and the absence of those closest to him were making him very lonely. His four sons were all serving in the armed forces, and Eleanor was usually away on tours ranging from military bases to service organizations. Louis Howe had died in 1936, followed by Roosevelt's mother in 1941. Then, late in 1944, the Reverend Endicott Peabody died. Roosevelt keenly felt the loss of this special man in his life. "The whole tone of things is going to be a bit different from now on," he wrote to Mrs. Peabody, "for I have leaned on the Rector in all these many years far more than most people know."

Harry Truman takes the oath of office a few hours after Roosevelt's death.

In March, under orders from his personal physician, Roosevelt left Washington for complete rest at the Little White House in Warm Springs, Georgia. After a few days of sun and relaxation, he seemed to improve. But the condition was only temporary. On April 12, 1945, he spent the morning reading the newspaper and working on his stamp collection. In the afternoon, not long after he began to pose for a portrait being painted of him, he complained of a "terrific headache" and slumped over. Four hours later he was dead of a broken blood vessel in the brain. Vice-President Harry S. Truman now took over the awesome duties of running a wartime government.

Franklin D. Roosevelt's funeral procession proceeds toward the Capitol, April 14, 1945.

Chapter 10

An Unfinished Peace

Franklin D. Roosevelt died before completing his fourth term as president and before seeing the end of the war. Although the Nazi empire was crumbling, Roosevelt would never experience the ultimate fulfillment of this final victory. Eleanor would now have to champion his special gift to the world, the United Nations.

Roosevelt was not the only national leader to die that April. Mussolini was shot in Italy on April 28. Two days later Hitler committed suicide in an underground bunker in Berlin. Three powerful men, whose desire for power had brought them together in world conflict, were dead. Less than a week after Hitler's suicide, the European war was over. On May 8, 1945, Victory in Europe (V-E) Day, Germany signed an unconditional surrender.

Still, the war continued in Asia. To shorten it and reduce the number of deaths the Allies would sustain, acting president Truman made a decision to drop two atomic bombs on key cities in Japan. (Development of the atomic bomb had actually begun in 1941 at Roosevelt's order.) On August 6 and 9, 1945, Hiroshima and Nagasaki were destroyed. About 107,000 people were killed and 128,000 were burned from radiation. On August 14, 1945, after great loss of human life, Japan surrendered.

World War II had come to an end. So had the leadership of a man who had become an American institution. Indeed, FDR had transformed not only the world of his own generation but that of future generations as well.

Institutions created by Roosevelt to prevent another Great Depression still exist today—regulation of the stock market, price controls on agricultural products, housing regulations, and federal insurance on bank deposits. Many of his social programs continue to shape life in America—social security, unemployment insurance, progressive income tax, minimum wages, maximum work hours, and mandatory retirement pensions.

Without a doubt, Roosevelt inspired confidence and vision. Yet many could see in him obvious contradictions. While he possessed the remarkable ambition of his cousin Theodore Roosevelt, he made enemies through his opposition to big business. He swore to uphold the idealism and civic duty of Endicott Peabody, but he thought nothing of packing the courts with his own judges. Born to model the high-society flair of his mother, he preferred to be identified with the common farmer and laborer. He appeared to espouse Eleanor's humanitarianism; yet he imprisoned Japanese-Americans, practically ignored the annihilation of Jews in Europe, and encouraged the development of the atomic bomb as a lethal weapon.

For better or for worse, no other president has had such a deep and lasting impact on life in America than has Franklin Delano Roosevelt. His personal courage in overcoming a physical handicap and converting tragedy into triumph will always be an inspiration to others.

Opposite page: FDR, an American classic

Chronology of American History

(Shaded area covers events in Franklin D. Roosevelt's lifetime.)

About A.D. 982 — Eric the Red, born in Norway, reaches Greenland in one of the first European voyages to North America.

About 1000 — Leif Ericson (Eric the Red's son) leads what is thought to be the first European expedition to mainland North America; Leif probably lands in Canada.

1492 — Christopher Columbus, seeking a sea route from Spain to the Far East, discovers the New World.

1497 — John Cabot reaches Canada in the first English voyage to North America.

1513 — Ponce de Léon explores Florida in search of the fabled Fountain of Youth.

1519-1521 — Hernando Cortés of Spain conquers Mexico.

1534 — French explorers led by Jacques Cartier enter the Gulf of St. Lawrence in Canada.

1540 — Spanish explorer Francisco Coronado begins exploring the American Southwest, seeking the riches of the mythical Seven Cities of Cibola.

1565 — St. Augustine, Florida, the first permanent European town in what is now the United States, is founded by the Spanish.

1607 — Jamestown, Virginia, is founded, the first permanent English town in the present-day U.S.

1608 — Frenchman Samuel de Champlain founds the village of Quebec, Canada.

1609 — Henry Hudson explores the eastern coast of present-day U.S. for the Netherlands; the Dutch then claim parts of New York, New Jersey, Delaware, and Connecticut and name the area New Netherland.

1619 — The English colonies' first shipment of black slaves arrives in Jamestown.

1620 — English Pilgrims found Massachusetts' first permanent town at Plymouth.

1621 — Massachusetts Pilgrims and Indians hold the famous first Thanksgiving feast in colonial America.

1623 — Colonization of New Hampshire is begun by the English.

1624 — Colonization of present-day New York State is begun by the Dutch at Fort Orange (Albany).

1625 — The Dutch start building New Amsterdam (now New York City).

1630 — The town of Boston, Massachusetts, is founded by the English Puritans.

1633 — Colonization of Connecticut is begun by the English.

1634 — Colonization of Maryland is begun by the English.

1636 — Harvard, the colonies' first college, is founded in Massachusetts. Rhode Island colonization begins when Englishman Roger Williams founds Providence.

1638 — Delaware colonization begins as Swedes build Fort Christina at present-day Wilmington.

1640 — Stephen Daye of Cambridge, Massachusetts prints *The Bay Psalm Book*, the first English-language book published in what is now the U.S.

1643 — Swedish settlers begin colonizing Pennsylvania.

About 1650 — North Carolina is colonized by Virginia settlers.

1660 — New Jersey colonization is begun by the Dutch at present-day Jersey City.

1670 — South Carolina colonization is begun by the English near Charleston.

1673 — Jacques Marquette and Louis Jolliet explore the upper Mississippi River for France.

1682—Philadelphia, Pennsylvania, is settled. La Salle explores Mississippi River all the way to its mouth in Louisiana and claims the whole Mississippi Valley for France.

1693—College of William and Mary is founded in Williamsburg, Virginia.

1700—Colonial population is about 250,000.

1703—Benjamin Franklin is born in Boston.

1732—George Washington, first president of the U.S., is born in Westmoreland County, Virginia.

1733—James Oglethorpe founds Savannah, Georgia; Georgia is established as the thirteenth colony.

1735—John Adams, second president of the U.S., is born in Braintree, Massachusetts.

1737—William Byrd founds Richmond, Virginia.

1738—British troops are sent to Georgia over border dispute with Spain.

1739—Black insurrection takes place in South Carolina.

1740—English Parliament passes act allowing naturalization of immigrants to American colonies after seven-year residence.

1743—Thomas Jefferson is born in Albemarle County, Virginia. Benjamin Franklin retires at age thirty-seven to devote himself to scientific inquiries and public service.

1744—King George's War begins; France joins war effort against England.

1745—During King George's War, France raids settlements in Maine and New York.

1747—Classes begin at Princeton College in New Jersey.

1748—The Treaty of Aix-la-Chapelle concludes King George's War.

1749—Parliament legally recognizes slavery in colonies and the inauguration of the plantation system in the South. George Washington becomes the surveyor for Culpepper County in Virginia.

1750—Thomas Walker passes through and names Cumberland Gap on his way toward Kentucky region. Colonial population is about 1,200,000.

1751—James Madison, fourth president of the U.S., is born in Port Conway, Virginia. English Parliament passes Currency Act, banning New England colonies from issuing paper money. George Washington travels to Barbados.

1752—Pennsylvania Hospital, the first general hospital in the colonies, is founded in Philadelphia. Benjamin Franklin uses a kite in a thunderstorm to demonstrate that lightning is a form of electricity.

1753—George Washington delivers command that the French withdraw from the Ohio River Valley; French disregard the demand. Colonial population is about 1,328,000.

1754—French and Indian War begins (extends to Europe as the Seven Years' War). Washington surrenders at Fort Necessity.

1755—French and Indians ambush Braddock. Washington becomes commander of Virginia troops.

1756—England declares war on France.

1758—James Monroe, fifth president of the U.S., is born in Westmoreland County, Virginia.

1759—Cherokee Indian war begins in southern colonies; hostilities extend to 1761. George Washington marries Martha Dandridge Custis.

1760—George III becomes king of England. Colonial population is about 1,600,000.

1762—England declares war on Spain.

1763—Treaty of Paris concludes the French and Indian War and the Seven Years' War. England gains Canada and most other French lands east of the Mississippi River.

1764—British pass the Sugar Act to gain tax money from the colonists. The issue of taxation without representation is first introduced in Boston. John Adams marries Abigail Smith.

1765—Stamp Act goes into effect in the colonies. Business virtually stops as almost all colonists refuse to use the stamps.

1766—British repeal the Stamp Act.

1767—John Quincy Adams, sixth president of the U.S. and son of second president John Adams, is born in Braintree, Massachusetts. Andrew Jackson, seventh president of the U.S., is born in Waxhaw settlement, South Carolina.

1769—Daniel Boone sights the Kentucky Territory.

1770—In the Boston Massacre, British soldiers kill five colonists and injure six. Townshend Acts are repealed, thus eliminating all duties on imports to the colonies except tea.

1771—Benjamin Franklin begins his autobiography, a work that he will never complete. The North Carolina assembly passes the "Bloody Act," which makes rioters guilty of treason.

1772—Samuel Adams rouses colonists to consider British threats to self-government.

1773—English Parliament passes the Tea Act. Colonists dressed as Mohawk Indians board British tea ships and toss 342 casks of tea into the water in what becomes known as the Boston Tea Party. William Henry Harrison is born in Charles City County, Virginia.

1774—British close the port of Boston to punish the city for the Boston Tea Party. First Continental Congress convenes in Philadelphia.

1775—American Revolution begins with battles of Lexington and Concord, Massachusetts. Second Continental Congress opens in Philadelphia. George Washington becomes commander-in-chief of the Continental army.

1776—Declaration of Independence is adopted on July 4.

1777—Congress adopts the American flag with thirteen stars and thirteen stripes. John Adams is sent to France to negotiate peace treaty.

1778—France declares war against Great Britain and becomes U.S. ally.

1779—British surrender to Americans at Vincennes. Thomas Jefferson is elected governor of Virginia. James Madison is elected to the Continental Congress.

1780—Benedict Arnold, first American traitor, defects to the British.

1781—Articles of Confederation go into effect. Cornwallis surrenders to George Washington at Yorktown, ending the American Revolution.

1782—American commissioners, including John Adams, sign peace treaty with British in Paris. Thomas Jefferson's wife, Martha, dies. Martin Van Buren is born in Kinderhook, New York.

1784—Zachary Taylor is born near Barboursville, Virginia.

1785—Congress adopts the dollar as the unit of currency. John Adams is made minister to Great Britain. Thomas Jefferson is appointed minister to France.

1786—Shays's Rebellion begins in Massachusetts.

1787—Constitutional Convention assembles in Philadelphia, with George Washington presiding; U.S. Constitution is adopted. Delaware, New Jersey, and Pennsylvania become states.

1788—Virginia, South Carolina, New York, Connecticut, New Hampshire, Maryland, and Massachusetts become states. U.S. Constitution is ratified. New York City is declared U.S. capital.

1789—Presidential electors elect George Washington and John Adams as first president and vice-president. Thomas Jefferson is appointed secretary of state. North Carolina becomes a state. French Revolution begins.

1790—Supreme Court meets for the first time. Rhode Island becomes a state. First national census in the U.S. counts 3,929,214 persons. John Tyler is born in Charles City County, Virginia.

1791—Vermont enters the Union. U.S. Bill of Rights, the first ten amendments to the Constitution, goes into effect. District of Columbia is established. James Buchanan is born in Stony Batter, Pennsylvania.

1792—Thomas Paine publishes *The Rights of Man.* Kentucky becomes a state. Two political parties are formed in the U.S., Federalist and Republican. Washington is elected to a second term, with Adams as vice-president.

1793—War between France and Britain begins; U.S. declares neutrality. Eli Whitney invents the cotton gin; cotton production and slave labor increase in the South.

1794—Eleventh Amendment to the Constitution is passed, limiting federal courts' power. "Whiskey Rebellion" in Pennsylvania protests federal whiskey tax. James Madison marries Dolley Payne Todd.

1795—George Washington signs the Jay Treaty with Great Britain. Treaty of San Lorenzo, between U.S. and Spain, settles Florida boundary and gives U.S. right to navigate the Mississippi. James Polk is born near Pineville, North Carolina.

1796—Tennessee enters the Union. Washington gives his Farewell Address, refusing a third presidential term. John Adams is elected president and Thomas Jefferson vice-president.

1797—Adams recommends defense measures against possible war with France. Napoleon Bonaparte and his army march against Austrians in Italy. U.S. population is about 4,900,000.

1798—Washington is named commander-in-chief of the U.S. Army. Department of the Navy is created. Alien and Sedition Acts are passed. Napoleon's troops invade Egypt and Switzerland.

1799—George Washington dies at Mount Vernon, New York. James Monroe is elected governor of Virginia. French Revolution ends. Napoleon becomes ruler of France.

1800—Thomas Jefferson and Aaron Burr tie for president. U.S. capital is moved from Philadelphia to Washington, D.C. The White House is built as presidents' home. Spain returns Louisiana to France. Millard Fillmore is born in Locke, New York.

1801—After thirty-six ballots, House of Representatives elects Thomas Jefferson president, making Burr vice-president. James Madison is named secretary of state.

1802—Congress abolishes excise taxes. U.S. Military Academy is founded at West Point, New York.

1803—Ohio enters the Union. Louisiana Purchase treaty is signed with France, greatly expanding U.S. territory.

1804—Twelfth Amendment to the Constitution rules that president and vice-president be elected separately. Alexander Hamilton is killed by Vice-President Aaron Burr in a duel. Orleans Territory is established. Napoleon crowns himself emperor of France. Franklin Pierce is born in Hillsborough Lower Village, New Hampshire.

1805—Thomas Jefferson begins his second term as president. Lewis and Clark expedition reaches the Pacific Ocean.

1806—Coinage of silver dollars is stopped; resumes in 1836.

1807—Aaron Burr is acquitted in treason trial. Embargo Act closes U.S. ports to trade.

1808—James Madison is elected president. Congress outlaws importing slaves from Africa. Andrew Johnson is born in Raleigh, North Carolina.

1809—Abraham Lincoln is born near Hodgenville, Kentucky.

1810—U.S. population is 7,240,000.

1811—William Henry Harrison defeats Indians at Tippecanoe. Monroe is named secretary of state.

1812—Louisiana becomes a state. U.S. declares war on Britain (War of 1812). James Madison is reelected president. Napoleon invades Russia.

1813—British forces take Fort Niagara and Buffalo, New York.

1814—Francis Scott Key writes "The Star-Spangled Banner." British troops burn much of Washington, D.C., including the White House. Treaty of Ghent ends War of 1812. James Monroe becomes secretary of war.

1815—Napoleon meets his final defeat at Battle of Waterloo.

1816—James Monroe is elected president. Indiana becomes a state.

1817—Mississippi becomes a state. Construction on Erie Canal begins.

1818—Illinois enters the Union. The present thirteen-stripe flag is adopted. Border between U.S. and Canada is agreed upon.

1819—Alabama becomes a state. U.S. purchases Florida from Spain. Thomas Jefferson establishes the University of Virginia.

1820—James Monroe is reelected. In the Missouri Compromise, Maine enters the Union as a free (non-slave) state.

1821—Missouri enters the Union as a slave state. Santa Fe Trail opens the American Southwest. Mexico declares independence from Spain. Napoleon Bonaparte dies.

1822—U.S. recognizes Mexico and Colombia. Liberia in Africa is founded as a home for freed slaves. Ulysses S. Grant is born in Point Pleasant, Ohio. Rutherford B. Hayes is born in Delaware, Ohio.

1823—Monroe Doctrine closes North and South America to European colonizing or invasion.

1824—House of Representatives elects John Quincy Adams president when none of the four candidates wins a majority in national election. Mexico becomes a republic.

1825—Erie Canal is opened. U.S. population is 11,300,000.

1826—Thomas Jefferson and John Adams both die on July 4, the fiftieth anniversary of the Declaration of Independence.

1828—Andrew Jackson is elected president. Tariff of Abominations is passed, cutting imports.

1829—James Madison attends Virginia's constitutional convention. Slavery is abolished in Mexico. Chester A. Arthur is born in Fairfield, Vermont.

1830—Indian Removal Act to resettle Indians west of the Mississippi is approved.

1831—James Monroe dies in New York City. James A. Garfield is born in Orange, Ohio. Cyrus McCormick develops his reaper.

1832—Andrew Jackson, nominated by the new Democratic Party, is reelected president.

1833—Britain abolishes slavery in its colonies. Benjamin Harrison is born in North Bend, Ohio.

1835—Federal government becomes debt-free for the first time.

1836—Martin Van Buren becomes president. Texas wins independence from Mexico. Arkansas joins the Union. James Madison dies at Montpelier, Virginia.

1837—Michigan enters the Union. U.S. population is 15,900,000. Grover Cleveland is born in Caldwell, New Jersey.

1840—William Henry Harrison is elected president.

1841—President Harrison dies in Washington, D.C., one month after inauguration. Vice-President John Tyler succeeds him.

1843—William McKinley is born in Niles, Ohio.

1844—James Knox Polk is elected president. Samuel Morse sends first telegraphic message.

1845—Texas and Florida become states. Potato famine in Ireland causes massive emigration from Ireland to U.S. Andrew Jackson dies near Nashville, Tennessee.

1846—Iowa enters the Union. War with Mexico begins.

1847—U.S. captures Mexico City.

1848—John Quincy Adams dies in Washington, D.C. Zachary Taylor becomes president. Treaty of Guadalupe Hidalgo ends Mexico-U.S. war. Wisconsin becomes a state.

1849—James Polk dies in Nashville, Tennessee.

1850—President Taylor dies in Washington, D.C.; Vice-President Millard Fillmore succeeds him. California enters the Union, breaking tie between slave and free states.

1852—Franklin Pierce is elected president.

1853—Gadsden Purchase transfers Mexican territory to U.S.

1854—"War for Bleeding Kansas" is fought between slave and free states.

1855—Czar Nicholas I of Russia dies, succeeded by Alexander II.

1856—James Buchanan is elected president. In Massacre of Potawatomi Creek, Kansas-slavers are murdered by free-staters. Woodrow Wilson is born in Staunton, Virginia.

1857—William Howard Taft is born in Cincinnati, Ohio.

1858—Minnesota enters the Union. Theodore Roosevelt is born in New York City.

1859—Oregon becomes a state.

1860—Abraham Lincoln is elected president; South Carolina secedes from the Union in protest.

1861—Arkansas, Tennessee, North Carolina, and Virginia secede. Kansas enters the Union as a free state. Civil War begins.

1862—Union forces capture Fort Henry, Roanoke Island, Fort Donelson, Jacksonville, and New Orleans; Union armies are defeated at the battles of Bull Run and Fredericksburg. Martin Van Buren dies in Kinderhook, New York. John Tyler dies near Charles City, Virginia.

1863—Lincoln issues Emancipation Proclamation: all slaves held in rebelling territories are declared free. West Virginia becomes a state.

1864—Abraham Lincoln is reelected. Nevada becomes a state.

1865—Lincoln is assassinated in Washington, D.C., and succeeded by Andrew Johnson. U.S. Civil War ends on May 26. Thirteenth Amendment abolishes slavery. Warren G. Harding is born in Blooming Grove, Ohio.

1867—Nebraska becomes a state. U.S. buys Alaska from Russia for $7,200,000. Reconstruction Acts are passed.

1868—President Johnson is impeached for violating Tenure of Office Act, but is acquitted by Senate. Ulysses S. Grant is elected president. Fourteenth Amendment prohibits voting discrimination. James Buchanan dies in Lancaster, Pennsylvania.

1869—Franklin Pierce dies in Concord, New Hampshire.

1870—Fifteenth Amendment gives blacks the right to vote.

1872—Grant is reelected over Horace Greeley. General Amnesty Act pardons ex-Confederates. Calvin Coolidge is born in Plymouth Notch, Vermont.

1874—Millard Fillmore dies in Buffalo, New York. Herbert Hoover is born in West Branch, Iowa.

1875—Andrew Johnson dies in Carter's Station, Tennessee.

1876—Colorado enters the Union. "Custer's last stand": he and his men are massacred by Sioux Indians at Little Big Horn, Montana.

1877—Rutherford B. Hayes is elected president as all disputed votes are awarded to him.

1880—James A. Garfield is elected president.

1881—President Garfield is assassinated and dies in Elberon, New Jersey. Vice-President Chester A. Arthur succeeds him.

1882—U.S. bans Chinese immigration. Franklin D. Roosevelt is born in Hyde Park, New York.

1884—Grover Cleveland is elected president. Harry S. Truman is born in Lamar, Missouri.

1885—Ulysses S. Grant dies in Mount McGregor, New York.

1886—Statue of Liberty is dedicated. Chester A. Arthur dies in New York City.

1888—Benjamin Harrison is elected president.

1889—North Dakota, South Dakota, Washington, and Montana become states.

1890—Dwight D. Eisenhower is born in Denison, Texas. Idaho and Wyoming become states.

1892—Grover Cleveland is elected president.

1893—Rutherford B. Hayes dies in Fremont, Ohio.

1896—William McKinley is elected president. Utah becomes a state.

1898—U.S. declares war on Spain over Cuba.

1900—McKinley is reelected. Boxer Rebellion against foreigners in China begins.

1901—McKinley is assassinated by anarchist Leon Czolgosz in Buffalo, New York; Theodore Roosevelt becomes president. Benjamin Harrison dies in Indianapolis, Indiana.

1902—U.S. acquires perpetual control over Panama Canal.

1903—Alaskan frontier is settled.

1904—Russian-Japanese War breaks out. Theodore Roosevelt wins presidential election.

1905—Treaty of Portsmouth signed, ending Russian-Japanese War.

1906—U.S. troops occupy Cuba.

1907—President Roosevelt bars all Japanese immigration. Oklahoma enters the Union.

1908—William Howard Taft becomes president. Grover Cleveland dies in Princeton, New Jersey. Lyndon B. Johnson is born near Stonewall, Texas.

1909—NAACP is founded under W.E.B. DuBois

1910—China abolishes slavery.

1911—Chinese Revolution begins. Ronald Reagan is born in Tampico, Illinois.

1912—Woodrow Wilson is elected president. Arizona and New Mexico become states.

1913—Federal income tax is introduced in U.S. through the Sixteenth Amendment. Richard Nixon is born in Yorba Linda, California. Gerald Ford is born in Omaha, Nebraska.

1914—World War I begins.

1915—British liner *Lusitania* is sunk by German submarine.

1916—Wilson is reelected president.

1917—U.S. breaks diplomatic relations with Germany. Czar Nicholas of Russia abdicates as revolution begins. U.S. declares war on Austria-Hungary. John F. Kennedy is born in Brookline, Massachusetts.

1918—Wilson proclaims "Fourteen Points" as war aims. On November 11, armistice is signed between Allies and Germany.

1919—Eighteenth Amendment prohibits sale and manufacture of intoxicating liquors. Wilson presides over first League of Nations; wins Nobel Peace Prize. Theodore Roosevelt dies in Oyster Bay, New York.

1920—Nineteenth Amendment (women's suffrage) is passed. Warren Harding is elected president.

1921—Adolf Hitler's stormtroopers begin to terrorize political opponents.

1922—Irish Free State is established. Soviet states form USSR. Benito Mussolini forms Fascist government in Italy.

1923—President Harding dies in San Francisco, California; he is succeeded by Vice-President Calvin Coolidge.

1924—Coolidge is elected president. Woodrow Wilson dies in Washington, D.C. James Carter is born in Plains, Georgia. George Bush is born in Milton, Massachusetts.

1925—Hitler reorganizes Nazi Party and publishes first volume of *Mein Kampf.*

1926—Fascist youth organizations founded in Germany and Italy. Republic of Lebanon proclaimed.

1927—Stalin becomes Soviet dictator. Economic conference in Geneva attended by fifty-two nations.

1928—Herbert Hoover is elected president. U.S. and many other nations sign Kellogg-Briand pacts to outlaw war.

1929—Stock prices in New York crash on "Black Thursday"; the Great Depression begins.

1930—Bank of U.S. and its many branches close (most significant bank failure of the year). William Howard Taft dies in Washington, D.C.

1931—Emigration from U.S. exceeds immigration for first time as Depression deepens.

1932—Franklin D. Roosevelt wins presidential election in a Democratic landslide.

1933—First concentration camps are erected in Germany. U.S. recognizes USSR and resumes trade. Twenty-First Amendment repeals prohibition. Calvin Coolidge dies in Northampton, Massachusetts.

1934—Severe dust storms hit Plains states. President Roosevelt passes U.S. Social Security Act.

1936—Roosevelt is reelected. Spanish Civil War begins. Hitler and Mussolini form Rome-Berlin Axis.

1937—Roosevelt signs Neutrality Act.

1938—Roosevelt sends appeal to Hitler and Mussolini to settle European problems amicably.

1939—Germany takes over Czechoslovakia and invades Poland, starting World War II.

1940—Roosevelt is reelected for a third term.

1941—Japan bombs Pearl Harbor, U.S. declares war on Japan. Germany and Italy declare war on U.S.; U.S. then declares war on them.

1942—Allies agree not to make separate peace treaties with the enemies. U.S. government transfers more than 100,000 Nisei (Japanese-Americans) from west coast to inland concentration camps.

1943—Allied bombings of Germany begin.

1944—Roosevelt is reelected for a fourth term. Allied forces invade Normandy on D-Day.

1945—President Franklin D. Roosevelt dies in Warm Springs, Georgia; Vice-President Harry S. Truman succeeds him. Mussolini is killed; Hitler commits suicide. Germany surrenders. U.S. drops atomic bomb on Hiroshima; Japan surrenders: end of World War II.

1946—U.N. General Assembly holds its first session in London. Peace conference of twenty-one nations is held in Paris.

1947—Peace treaties are signed in Paris. "Cold War" is in full swing.

1948—U.S. passes Marshall Plan Act, providing $17 billion in aid for Europe. U.S. recognizes new nation of Israel. India and Pakistan become free of British rule. Truman is elected president.

1949—Republic of Eire is proclaimed in Dublin. Russia blocks land route access from Western Germany to Berlin; airlift begins. U.S., France, and Britain agree to merge their zones of occupation in West Germany. Apartheid program begins in South Africa.

1950—Riots in Johannesburg, South Africa, against apartheid. North Korea invades South Korea. U.N. forces land in South Korea and recapture Seoul.

1951—Twenty-Second Amendment limits president to two terms.

1952—Dwight D. Eisenhower resigns as supreme commander in Europe and is elected president.

1953—Stalin dies; struggle for power in Russia follows. Rosenbergs are executed for espionage.

1954—U.S. and Japan sign mutual defense agreement.

1955—Blacks in Montgomery, Alabama, boycott segregated bus lines.

1956—Eisenhower is reelected president. Soviet troops march into Hungary.

1957—U.S. agrees to withdraw ground forces from Japan. Russia launches first satellite, *Sputnik*.

1958—European Common Market comes into being. Fidel Castro begins war against Batista government in Cuba.

1959—Alaska becomes the forty-ninth state. Hawaii becomes fiftieth state. Castro becomes premier of Cuba. De Gaulle is proclaimed president of the Fifth Republic of France.

1960—Historic debates between Senator John F. Kennedy and Vice-President Richard Nixon are televised. Kennedy is elected president. Brezhnev becomes president of USSR.

1961—Berlin Wall is constructed. Kennedy and Khrushchev confer in Vienna. In Bay of Pigs incident, Cubans trained by CIA attempt to overthrow Castro.

1962—U.S. military council is established in South Vietnam.

1963—Riots and beatings by police and whites mark civil rights demonstrations in Birmingham, Alabama; 30,000 troops are called out, Martin Luther King, Jr., is arrested. Freedom marchers descend on Washington, D.C., to demonstrate. President Kennedy is assassinated in Dallas, Texas; Vice-President Lyndon B. Johnson is sworn in as president.

1964—U.S. aircraft bomb North Vietnam. Johnson is elected president. Herbert Hoover dies in New York City.

1965—U.S. combat troops arrive in South Vietnam.

1966—Thousands protest U.S. policy in Vietnam. National Guard quells race riots in Chicago.

1967—Six-Day War between Israel and Arab nations.

1968—Martin Luther King, Jr., is assassinated in Memphis, Tennessee. Senator Robert Kennedy is assassinated in Los Angeles. Riots and police brutality take place at Democratic National Convention in Chicago. Richard Nixon is elected president. Czechoslovakia is invaded by Soviet troops.

1969—Dwight D. Eisenhower dies in Washington, D.C. Hundreds of thousands of people in several U.S. cities demonstrate against Vietnam War.

1970—Four Vietnam War protesters are killed by National Guardsmen at Kent State University in Ohio.

1971—Twenty-Sixth Amendment allows eighteen-year-olds to vote.

1972—Nixon visits Communist China; is reelected president in near-record landslide. Watergate affair begins when five men are arrested in the Watergate hotel complex in Washington, D.C. Nixon announces resignations of aides Haldeman, Ehrlichman, and Dean and Attorney General Kleindienst as a result of Watergate-related charges. Harry S. Truman dies in Kansas City, Missouri.

1973—Vice-President Spiro Agnew resigns; Gerald Ford is named vice-president. Vietnam peace treaty is formally approved after nineteen months of negotiations. Lyndon B. Johnson dies in San Antonio, Texas.

1974—As a result of Watergate cover-up, impeachment is considered; Nixon resigns and Ford becomes president. Ford pardons Nixon and grants limited amnesty to Vietnam War draft evaders and military deserters.

1975—U.S. civilians are evacuated from Saigon, South Vietnam, as Communist forces complete takeover of South Vietnam.

1976—U.S. celebrates its Bicentennial. James Earl Carter becomes president.

1977—Carter pardons most Vietnam draft evaders, numbering some 10,000.

1980—Ronald Reagan is elected president.

1981—President Reagan is shot in the chest in assassination attempt. Sandra Day O'Connor is appointed first woman justice of the Supreme Court.

1983—U.S. troops invade island of Grenada.

1984—Reagan is reelected president. Democratic candidate Walter Mondale's running mate, Geraldine Ferraro, is the first woman selected for vice-president by a major U.S. political party.

1985—Soviet Communist Party secretary Konstantin Chernenko dies; Mikhail Gorbachev succeeds him. U.S. and Soviet officials discuss arms control in Geneva. Reagan and Gorbachev hold summit conference in Geneva. Racial tensions accelerate in South Africa.

1986—Space shuttle *Challenger* explodes shortly after takeoff; crew of seven dies. U.S. bombs bases in Libya. Corazon Aquino defeats Ferdinand Marcos in Philippine presidential election.

1987—Iraqi missile rips the U.S. frigate *Stark* in the Persian Gulf, killing thirty-seven American sailors. Congress holds hearings to investigate sale of U.S. arms to Iran to finance Nicaraguan *contra* movement.

1988—President Reagan and Soviet leader Gorbachev sign INF treaty, eliminating intermediate nuclear forces. Severe drought sweeps the United States. George Bush is elected president.

1989—East Germany opens Berlin Wall, allowing citizens free exit. Communists lose control of governments in Poland, Romania, and Czechoslovakia. Chinese troops massacre over 1,000 pro-democracy student demonstrators in Beijing's Tiananmen Square.

1990—Iraq annexes Kuwait, provoking the threat of war. East and West Germany are reunited. The Cold War between the United States and the Soviet Union comes to a close. Several Soviet republics make moves toward independence.

1991—Backed by a coalition of members of the United Nations, U.S. troops drive Iraqis from Kuwait. Latvia, Lithuania, and Estonia withdraw from the USSR. The Soviet Union dissolves as its republics secede to form a Commonwealth of Independent States.

1992—U.N. forces fail to stop fighting in territories of former Yugoslavia. More than fifty people are killed and more than six hundred buildings burned in rioting in Los Angeles. U.S. unemployment reaches eight-year high. Hurricane Andrew devastates southern Florida and parts of Louisiana. International relief supplies and troops are sent to combat famine and violence in Somalia.

1993—U.S.-led forces use airplanes and missiles to attack military targets in Iraq. William Jefferson Clinton becomes the forty-second U.S. president.

1994—Richard M. Nixon dies in New York City.

Index

Page numbers in boldface type indicate illustrations.

Albany, New York, 34
Agricultural Adjustment Agency (AAA), 57
Arizona, 75
Arkansas, 75
Army, U.S., 78
"Arsenal of Democracy," 68
Asia, 61, 63, 78, 87
Atlantic Charter, 67
atomic bombs, 87
Austria, 64
Axis powers, 63, 66, 70, 76, 78
banking, 7, 46, **48**, 49, 53-55, 58, 88
Belgium, 64
Berlin, Germany, 82, 87
Bethune, Mary McLeod, 60
blacks, 60, 75, **80**
Boy Scouts, **40**, 41
cabinets, Roosevelt's, 53, 60
California, 75
Campobello (island, Canada), **4**, 12, 41
Capitol, **86**
cartoons, **58, 59**
characteristics, Roosevelt's, 9, 18, 53, 88
Chicago, Illinois, 50, 56
childhood, Roosevelt's, 11-14, 16
China, 76
Churchill, Winston, 67, **67**, 68, 76, 81, **81**, 82
civil rights, 60
Civilian Conservation Corps (CCC), 56
Columbia Law School, 28, 31, 33
concentration camps, 64
Congress, U.S., 51, 53, 55, 68, 73
conservation programs, 51
Constitution, U.S., 28
Coolidge, Calvin, 39
Cox, James M., 37-38, **38**
credit, 46, 48, 53
Crimson (Harvard University newspaper), 23
Cuba, 17
Czechoslovakia, 64
D-Day, 82
death camps, 64
death of Roosevelt, 85, **86**, 87
debate team, 17-18
Declaration of Independence, 24, 28
Delaware and Hudson Railway, 11
Democratic party, 33, 37, 43, 45, 58, 60, 82
draft, military, 68
economic aid programs, 51
economy, U.S., 7-9, 46, 49-51, 59
education, Roosevelt's, 12-13, 16-17, 18, **18**, 19, 21-23, 28, 31
Eisenhower, Dwight D., 78, 82

Emergency Banking Act, 53
England, 64, 66-67, 69, 71, 73, 76
Europe, 11-12, 26, 28, 36, 61, 63-64, 68, 78, 81, 87-88
farming, 7, 34-35, 57, 76
Federal Deposit Insurance Corporation (FDIC), 57
Federal Reserve System, 53
"Fireside Chats," 54, 68-69
France, 64, 66-67, 69-70, 81
French Indochina, 70
Germany, 36, 63-64, 67, 69-70, 73, 78, 80-82, 87
governorship, New York, 33, 45-46, 49-50
Grand Coulee Dam, Washington, 56
Great Britain. *See* England
Great Depression, **6**, 7, 8, **8**, 9, 49, 51, **54**, 58, 88
Groton School, 16, 17, **17**, 18, **18**, 19, 33
Grumman Wildcats (airplanes), **62**
Guam, 78
Half Moon (boat), 16
Harding, Warren G., 39
Harvard University, 21-22, **22**, 23, **23**, 33
Hawaiian Islands, 71
Hiroshima, Japan, 87
Hitler, Adolf, 63-64, **65**, 66, 69, 78, 80, 87
hobbies, Roosevelt's, 13-14, 16, 85
Hong Kong, 78
Hoover, Herbert, 8, 45, 51
Howe, Louis Henry, 35, 38, 43, 45, **51**, 84
Hudson River, New York, 11, 13, 16, 82
"Hundred Days," 55
Hyde Park, New York, 11, 14, 16, 24
illnesses, Roosevelt's, 9, 17-18, 35, 42
inauguration(s), Roosevelt's, 9, **9**, 19, 53, 82, **83**
industry, 7, 48, 76
Italy, 63, 66, 73, 80, 87
Japan, 63, 70-73, 78, 87
Japanese-Americans, 75-76, **77**, 88
Jewish persecution, 64, **65**, 88
La Guardia Airport, New York, 57
lend-lease policy, 68-70
Little White House, 85
Livingston, Philip, 24
Livingston, Robert, 24
London, England, 11, 66
MacArthur, Douglas, 78
map of Pearl Harbor, **71**
military: Canadian, 82; British, 78, 82; French, 82; German, 66, **66**, 78, 80; Japanese, 71-72; American, 72, 75-76, 78, **80**, 82, **83**

Mussolini, Benito, 63, 78, **79**, 80, 87
Nagasaki, Japan, 87
National Recovery Administration (NRA), 57
National Socialist Workers, 63
Navy, U.S., 17, 33, 35-37, 76
Nazi party, 63-64, 68, 87
New Deal, 50, 56-58
New Moon (boat), 16
New York, 11, 14, 16, 24, 28, 33-34, 41,
   45, 46, 49, 56
New York City, 11, 28, 41, 49
New York Herald (newspaper), 35
Nimitz, Chester, 78
Nisei (World War II regiment), 76
Normandy, France, 81
North Africa, 78
Oahu, Hawaii, 71-72
Operation Overlord, 82
Operation Torch, 78
Pacific Ocean, 71, 78
Paris, France, 11, 66
Peabody, Endicott, 16, 18-19, 28, 84, 88
Pearl Harbor, Hawaii, 71, **71**, 72-73, **73**, 75
Perkins, Frances, 60
Philippines, 78
Poland, 64
polio, 9, 42-43, 45
political corruption, 33-34
presidential elections, 35, 37-38, **38**, 45,
   50, **50**, 51, **61**
Public Works Administration (PWA), 56
public works program, 51
radio broadcasts, 7, 54
railroads, 38, 48
reforms, political and social, 34, 46, 55-56, 88
relief programs, 49, 51, **54**, 56, **56**, 57
relocation centers, 75, **77**
Republican party, 33, 39, 45
"Roaring Twenties," 48
Roosevelt, Anna (daughter), 28, **31**, **39**
Roosevelt, Anna Eleanor (wife), **5**, 24, **25**,
   26, **27**, 28, **29**, **30**, **31**, 34, 38, **39**, 41-
   43, 47, 60, **60**, 82, 84, 87, 88
Roosevelt, Elliott (son), 28, 84, 39
Roosevelt, Franklin D., pictures of, **2**, **5**, **9**,
   10, **12**, **13**, **14**, **15**, **17**, **18**, **19**, **20**, **22**,
   23, **25**, **31**, **32**, **34**, **35**, **37**, **38**, **39**, **40**,
   43, **44**, **47**, **49**, **50**, **51**, **52**, **55**, **67**, **74**,
   79, **81**, **83**, **84**, **89**

Roosevelt, Franklin, Jr. (son), 28, **39**, 43
Roosevelt, James (father), **10**, 11, **19**, 21
Roosevelt, James (son), 24, 28, **39**, 84
Roosevelt, John (son), 28, **39**, 84
Roosevelt, Sara Delano (mother), 11, 12,
   15, 21, 26, **27**, **39**
Roosevelt, Theodore (Teddy; cousin), 17,
   21, 26, 28, 33, 46, 88
Rough Riders, 17
Royal Air Force (RAF), England, 66
Russia. *See* Soviet Union
Securities and Exchange Commission
   (SEC), 57
Selective Training and Service Act, 68
Smith, Al, 43, 45
Social Security Act, 57
Southeast Asia, 71
Soviet Union, 69, 76, 80
Spanish-American War, 17
Stalin, Josef, 69, **69**, 81, **81**, 82
stock market, 46, 48-49, 88
Supreme Court, U.S., 58-59
Tammany Hall, 34
Tennessee Valley Authority, 57
Third Reich, 63
Tojo, Hideki (Japanese premier), **70**
Tokyo, Japan, 78
Truman, Harry, **84**, 85, **85**, 87
unemployment, 7, **8**, 53, 57
unemployment insurance, 49, 51, 56
unions, 57
United Nations, 81-82, 87
V-E day, 87
Vietnam, 70
Warm Springs, Georgia, 42-43, **43**, 85
Washington, 56
Washington, D.C., 36, 85
Washington, George, 24
weapons, 67-68, 76
White House, 19, 21, 26, 33, 35, 46, 54
Wilson, Woodrow, 35, **35**
women's rights, 34, 37, 75
workmen's compensation, 34
Works Projects Administration (WPA), **56**, 57
World War I, 36-37
World War II, **62**, 64, **65**, 66, **66**, 67-71,
   72, **72**, 73, **73**, 75-76, 78, **79**, 80, **80**,
   81-82, **83**, 87-88
Yalta, Russia, 82

About the Author

Alice Osinski is a Chicago-based free-lance writer and photo researcher. She holds a B.A. in the Social Sciences, with special coursework in American Indian Studies. After teaching American Indian children for seven years in Pine Ridge, South Dakota, and Gallup, New Mexico, Ms. Osinski launched her career in writing. She has developed bicultural curricula for alternative school programs in South Dakota and New Mexico. Her articles and children's stories have appeared in textbooks for D.C. Heath and Open Court. She has written several books for Childrens Press, including *Andrew Jackson* in the *Encyclopedia of Presidents* series.